GUIDED

*Life long self awareness techniques to
raise your vibration and bring
you more joy*

Theresa Porter

BALBOA.PRESS

A DIVISION OF HAY HOUSE

Balboa Press books may be ordered through booksellers or by contacting:

Balboa Press
A Division of Hay House
1663 Liberty Drive
Bloomington, IN 47403
www.balboapress.com
844-682-1282

Because of the dynamic nature of the Internet, any web addresses or
links contained in this book may have changed since publication and
may no longer be valid. The views expressed in this work are solely those
of the author and do not necessarily reflect the views of the publisher,
and the publisher hereby disclaims any responsibility for them.

The author of this book does not dispense medical advice or prescribe the use
of any technique as a form of treatment for physical, emotional, or medical
problems without the advice of a physician, either directly or indirectly. The
intent of the author is only to offer information of a general nature to help
you in your quest for emotional and spiritual well-being. In the event you use
any of the information in this book for yourself, which is your constitutional
right, the author and the publisher assume no responsibility for your actions.

Any people depicted in stock imagery provided by Getty Images are
models, and such images are being used for illustrative purposes only.
Certain stock imagery © Getty Images.

Print information available on the last page.

ISBN: 979-8-7652-4157-8 (sc)
ISBN: 979-8-7652-4159-2 (hc)
ISBN: 979-8-7652-4158-5 (e)

Library of Congress Control Number: 2023908146

Balboa Press rev. date: 04/27/2023

When writing this book, I told myself:
I will carefully curate this content so that
others can mindfully implement it.

As you do the work, Remind yourself:

What goes on in your mind is a direct reflection of what goes on in your waking world. What will your focus be?

Contents

Putting yourself to task

The question is not if somebody has issues but if you are willing to do something about your own. When you can work through your issues, everything else will seemingly work itself out. Everyone has unique challenges, but it always comes down to the attitude put forward that will determine the outcome. Remember, it's not just you, life happens, and things will be as amazing or depraving as you allow. Life is about breaking down the walls you thought were built for protection and realizing they are self-created barriers you don't need and are holding you back.

As you begin this journey of techniques that I've set out in a several-week program to assist you, allow any emotions that may come up to flow. Don't ignore them or push them down, as many of us are taught to do. Be sure to feel what comes, sit with it, and work through it. Stagnant and blocked energy, including unresolved hurts or traumatic events, as well as others within the body, can result in many illnesses or pains. Dealing with these will allow you to get your energy flowing and the blockages to simply dissipate over time.

Before beginning, It would be best practice to write out where you are and how you are feeling before embarking on this journey so that you can look back and see the progress you have made vs. where this journey is taking you, as well as creating and having a proper practice for release. Weekly journaling of where you are emotionally, mentally, and physically is highly recommended. Daily journaling would be even better, if possible, so that you can get a clear step-by-step view of what these practices have brought up and made you recognize within yourself and your surroundings. Doing this daily also allows you to release and express what's going on and what you are going through to assist in creating a "letting go" of sorts. Take the time to really recognize how you are doing and feeling, as well as what obstacles you have in your life. You are writing these feelings and emotions down as they come so that you can acknowledge them and work through them or past them. Feel the feels! What you are doing is creating your own accountability diary, for the more you continue and are consistent, the more you'll notice these practices getting easier and coming to you quicker. Key reminder, It'll get easier, all of it!

We can set mental barriers for ourselves when in the midst of a situation because of where we are and not being able to see the end result. "How can I be excited or happy even though I know the end result because I am in the mud or metaphorical quicksand of it all right now?". Well, if this is a question you're asking yourself, It's more common than you think, and you are definitely not the only one. The issue is just how unhealthy this mindset is. You have to make sure you aren't trying to find reasons why or validation as to why you're allowed to be in misery. Validating being able to say why you've earned the ability to be hurtful to yourself and/or others, why you deserve this and potentially more than others, why it's other people's reactions or actions that are at fault, and worse of all, why others need to hear and acknowledge your mental clutter and validate it for you is never going to help with getting you ahead of it all. It's hard to change the narrative when we haven't taken the time to slow down and focus first. Just as with anything else, this will take time, and you will learn along the way. You need to make sure you recognize what you are putting yourself through. You need to see what negative habits you have welcomed into your life and not refuse to acknowledge them for the simple fact that they have become familiar and what you are accustomed to because if everything is a struggle right now, it's not going to get better until a change is accepted. Now as important as this is, don't do this practice and at any point start to think that you are a terrible person because I promise you that you are most definitely not! It's just habits and learned behaviors, along with some choices that you have gotten yourself into. It's all in learning.

You need to work on finding happiness and recognize what you really have going on, or no matter what you do or don't do, where you go or not go, that bitterness, anger, sadness, depression, or other negative emotions you have will simply follow. As you go through these tasks and processes, try looking at all the people you grew up with and around. Is any of what you are doing now simply a habit, belief, view, or reaction that you picked up along the way? Use this knowledge to motivate yourself, to not place judgment on yourself or anyone else, or get yourself into a negative thought spiral. Work on not feeding into the belief of "It's easier to fall into the negative naturally" or "Our minds have a wired tendency to naturally be more negative than positive." This is what we have learned and chose to believe and repeat to ourselves. It takes more energy and effort, a conscious effort to be more positive. Our brains want to keep us smaller and safer as more and more events occur. But we can change this if we choose to. We just need to get through the negative and reteach our minds to our new and desired focuses. So start telling yourself that it's easier for you to fall into the positive. We have this inherent belief that we must search out the negative for survival but in today's world, that doesn't really apply, so we need to learn how we can leave that outgrown requirement where it belongs, and that is in the past.

As you begin, remember not to take on any stress or negative self-talk. This is all about the intention you are willing to put behind the processes and not the anxiety or the moments of "I can't do this." There's no right way, and there's no wrong way. There's no time expectation. It's about giving yourself time to learn and be patient through everything, no matter what may arise. As long as you are putting in the effort, you will see results. None of this is a race, so remember to breathe and work through in your own time as slowly as needed so that these implementations will be easier for your mind to accept and get behind, as this may be a new and foreign flow. You may even choose to extend one of the week's tasks for an extra week should you feel the need for more time. The only watchful eye that needs to be kept on a choice like this will be if you are doing this to truly further work on a task or if your fear of moving forward consciously or subconsciously wants to pull you back.

As you continue, you may start to have moments of realization and showing of emotions. This is your physical body releasing in order to allow you to raise your energetic vibration. Different things will come up for different people, and all of it is valid for each of you. Be sure you allow this to come to the surface and run its course as your mind and body are learning to process and move past. Do not stay in these moments. Simply understand them for what they are. Use your journaling to also assist in getting this energy out and learning how to forgive others and, most importantly yourself. If possible, in these high-emotion moments, you could take a shower.

Allow the water to run over you. As the water runs down your body, imagine it is helping pull these long-held and now resurfacing moments out of you to help clear and cleanse.

A bath to be able to stop and sit peacefully and calmly is also a great option. As you relax in the water, simply imagine it is helping by taking on the hurt of the moment and sweeping it down the drain with it once you are done.

As you keep going and keep pushing yourself, you will notice changes and will be able to recognize situations simply for what they were. Understanding those moments and the person they have allowed you to become should help with being grateful for those moments and the lessons and growth they have brought you. Even the moments and situations that we label as "bad" have brought us growth or can once we separate from the initial hurt caused. None of those situations can be erased, nor should you want them to be, as they are what helped to form and shape who you are today and the ability to assist others with your newfound knowledge should you want or be in a situation where you could. We can't maintain a negative eye toward these things and events. That view will never serve or assist us. We need to stop and ask ourselves, "Ok, what good can I take from this?". The wisdom it provided is truly priceless. Sometimes you just need to look a little harder for it.

Doing simple practices like the ones you are about to undertake is so important for self-awareness and overall growth. They are simple but, at the same time, huge for that needed and overdue recognition and prevention of continued self-sabotage that happens when trying to change what felt safe and what you believed protected you from the hurts, scares, and pushes into unknown territories. This is about learning what you want as your belief system and knowing how to reinforce that.

These are processes and skills you can continue throughout your life to maintain a higher level of joy and evaluation of what joy truly is for you. You will change over time, and so will your likes and dislikes. Creating a healthy acknowledgment and the ability to communicate now what joy is for and to you is vital for a happy and healthy life. Remember, you will get from this what you are willing to put into it.

The end goal of all of this is for you to have greater self-awareness and acknowledgment. For you to have worked through, or are well on your way to working through, different traumas, issues, and things that hold you back in life as well as cause blockages and unhealthy buildup in your human body. When you can allow yourself to be in a more positive frame of mind, it allows you to release negativity so that you can manifest and create what truly fills you.

If emotions can be displayed on a scale with the most negative at the bottom and the most love and joy-filled at the top and everything else in between, then this process and these practices are to help move you on that scale in every way possible away from those lower levels and shoot you up to make you a more positive and happier person overall. It's raising your vibration on this emotional scale.

Speaking vibrationally, if you want to raise up the vibrational scale, you need to let go of what holds you back from reaching those higher-up emotions. You need to be aware and accept changes as they come. Give thanks for each and every time it had with you and for what it taught you. Be grateful for the new things that will be coming before they are even here, like new people, things, places, events, opportunities, and so on.

When you start to work through your own storm of emotions, things will get better, I promise! As soon as you figure your own mind out, the rest will come because your world is merely a reflection of the current state of your mind.

Think of what you are about to embark on as someone going through rehabilitation, but instead of a person, it's your brain, and instead of alcohol or drugs, it's your thoughts and beliefs. When someone is going through rehab to get clean, they don't continue to hang out with drug dealers, addicts, and enablers. They come away from all of that and find a new group, support, friends, and a new system to function within. They don't return to where they were once they can see the harm it was causing. So as you start to self-recognize and are able to see what was toxic and can move away from it, you will also see those enablers and encouragers and dealers and other addicts fall away. Now, some may go out fighting harder than others, and you might need to remind yourself why you are doing this. Always remember that wherever you are on that emotional scale, things of that same vibration are what you are attracting. Is that really where you want to stay, or do you want to continue and raise yourself up?

Ask yourself what it is you want to resonate with. Maybe even allow this to be your first journaling step. Allowing it to open with the question of what it is you want and then break down where it is you truly are. Being brutally honest and stripping away any facade or walls that you've held with such importance is vital in getting to the real issues that have been left to build up or ignored to fester within you.

And with that, Let's do what we can to make sure we are not holding these traumas, disappointments, fury, and emotional flurries any longer. This process is going to be what you make of it. We all have choices to make regarding what kind of life we are going to live. Ask yourself, are you going to allow negativity to rule, or will you make this into everything it could be and more? Because you're the author of your own story and need to decide how you want to write it.

So, let's get started!

It's amongst the rubble that we are not lost but found, and our true beauty begins to flourish.

Week One

Finding White

THIS FIRST WEEK WILL CONSIST OF A SIMPLE YET POWERFUL practice before sleep, and upon waking that you will continue moving forward to optimize your quality of sleep and to get your days started with a light and positive vibe. This practice will help you by taking all the junk from your day and cleaning and clearing it out so that you aren't trying to get to sleep with a list of occurrences taking over your mind and potentially waking you throughout the night or even haunting your dreams. It will also help set your mind up for the day you are about to take on and its challenges ahead. It will put you in a more positive state to help attract more of the same.

For some, this may be very simple. For others, this may take a little more time and practice. Ultimately, it's not a race, and there's no wrong or right way that this can be completed as long as you are being easy on yourself and not putting too much thought into the process because it truly is basic. With time you will learn to calm your mind, if you haven't already, and complete this easily and happily.

This is a practice you will want to carry forward for ending and beginning your day as the benefits of this simple yet powerful exercise will begin to show themselves with regular use and become irresistible. So, don't stop at week one. Make sure that you work this into a daily routine. You'll thank yourself in the long run and realize managing an extra few minutes at the end of your day and before starting, is easier than some may think and more beneficial than you could envision.

Once implemented as a daily routine, It will assist in releasing your tension from the day (whether we know it's there or not) and also getting you started with a more happy and positive perspective.

Think of it as washing up before bed and getting ready in the morning or, even more similar, how you brush your teeth in the morning and at night.

So what is this practice? Let's get started!

Once you are ready for bed, under the sheets and wanting to drift off for the night, quickly take 10 minutes to sit up with your hands on your lap, and your eyes closed to imagine or picture white. This can be as simple as picturing a flower or a car in your mind, but instead of a familiar item, let it be a white piece of paper that slowly takes over your entire view or perhaps a white sheet slowly dropping down or being pulled up from below. It could even be white walls that are slowly closing in to meet. The ultimate goal is just to see white. Nothing less and nothing more.

If other thoughts pop into your mind, don't judge yourself or become frustrated. Remember to be easy on yourself as you learn to calm and focus your mind. As these thoughts come through, simply acknowledge the thought for what it is and move it along. Just tell yourself, "Oh, there's another thought," and continue with the task. Maybe even slipping in a smile.

So once your day is over and you've allowed yourself to relax under your sheets, Start with a nice deep breath. Make sure you continue breathing through the process, relax your muscles, and drop your shoulders and tongue from the roof of your mouth. Don't tense up, and be sure your whole body is relaxed. If you catch yourself tensing up, simply re-relax those muscles and take another nice deep breath. Roll your shoulders back and maybe even circle the neck to loosen it up. Hands resting nicely on your lap, begin to start picturing white. Do this for 10 minutes. Then you need just to lay back and drift off to sleep for the night.

In the morning, as soon as you wake, before getting out of bed and relieving your bladder, getting yourself a drink, or even checking your devices, make sure you simply sit up, place your hands on your lap, roll those shoulders back and maybe even circle the neck, take a deep breath, drop your tongue from the roof of your mouth and keep those eyes closed to begin the same process of picturing white for about 10 minutes. Once done, begin your day! If you are having trouble, which is very common at the beginning, you may even need to start with just seeing the word "White." Whatever gets you to the end goal is just fine! Tweaking the practice a bit is ok. You may even want to start with other visualizations and work your way into seeing white. Remember, the end goal is to visualize white. It doesn't matter how you get yourself there!

Here are a few visualization techniques I have used with clients that you can use if going straight into seeing white proves overly difficult, at least at the beginning. If you are practicing this with someone, you could read one of these techniques to each other as you start your journey. If embarking on this self-improvement journey on your own, simply read the practice you wish to try and lead yourself through it the best you can remember. Be sure that, in either case, you are taking the time to pre-read the techniques before using them. If reading them to someone, do so slowly and with a monotone voice. Also, as a side note, if you find yourself sneezing, burping, or hiccuping during this process, it is a completely normal method your body uses to release energy. Be sure not to allow this to throw you off and to simply refocus yourself each time. Self-judgment and doubt can be our biggest downfall when attempting to raise our emotional state.

Good luck, and don't give up!

Weekly task:

- Imagine white for 10 minutes before going to sleep and before getting out of bed in the morning

Technique 1

To assist in visualizing white

Place your hands on your lap, roll your shoulders back, circle your neck, take a deep breath, drop your tongue from the roof of your mouth, and allow your eyes to close gently on your next exhale.

Imagine yourself in your kitchen. It's the cleanest it has ever been! You're happy and relaxed. You look over and notice a beautiful vase with water in it sitting on the counter, but no flowers are in it.

You are now going to walk into your bedroom. Look around and notice if the bed is made. Do you see anything on the floor? Are the curtains open, or have they been closed?

Take another nice deep breath, and on your exhale, you hear a knock on the front door. Start making your way there. Take another nice big breath in once you are in front of your door, and as you exhale, reach out and open your door.

Recognize that a delivery person is holding a bouquet of beautiful big white flowers. They've already been trimmed and are ready to be placed in a vase! You now realize that the vase on your counter must have been for these and was pre-prepared for you. How nice!

Reach out and take the flowers as you thank the delivery person. Close the door and make your way to your kitchen. Place the flowers into the vase and take a moment to stare at them and simply admire their beauty. Notice how overly large and pure white the pedals are. Now with another deep breath in, slowly begin to lower down to smell the beautiful flowers. Keep your eyes open and let your breath out. The pedals are so large, and they are all you can see. They take up your entire view!

Should anything come along and distract you from these beautiful flowers, simply take another big breath and lean back into them. Enjoy the pure white pedals. Continue breathing and ensure your tongue is dropped from the roof of your mouth, and your shoulders are relaxed.

Technique 2

To assist in visualizing white

Place your hands on your lap, roll your shoulders back, circle your neck, take a deep breath, drop your tongue from the roof of your mouth, and allow your eyes to close gently on your next exhale.

Imagine yourself sitting in your living room. As you look around, you will start to notice that this is the cleanest your home has ever been! Take a moment to sit here and enjoy.

Take another nice big breath in, and as you exhale, stand up and walk to the exit. As you step outside, you realize that all around you is nothing but a lush, beautiful forest. Take a moment to breathe the beautiful, fresh, and clean air as you begin to walk to the back of your home. You are now going to notice that behind your home, there is an opening in the forest that leads to a beautiful path. Walk to this path.

Right before entering, Take a nice big breath in, and as you exhale, enter the forest. Feel the peace that surrounds you. Touch the trees as they pass. Look up to notice birds flying amongst the leaf-filled branches. As you drop your head down to see in front of you, notice that it is beaming with white light. As you get closer, the light gets brighter. Once you reach the end of the forest, you are surrounded by this beautiful white light. It is all you can see.

Should a noise from the forest distract you or take you from this beautiful white light, just turn your head back, take another nice big breath, and enjoy its warmth and beauty. Continue breathing and ensure your tongue is dropped from the roof of your mouth and your shoulders are relaxed.

Technique 3

To assist in visualizing white

Place your hands on your lap, roll your shoulders back, circle your neck, take a deep breath, drop your tongue from the roof of your mouth, and allow your eyes to close gently on your next exhale.

Imagine yourself walking through your home. It's the cleanest it's ever been. You are walking around just to enjoy it. As you walk into your kitchen, you notice that there is an extra door. It's a beautiful white door. Even though you've never seen it, it makes you happy. You can tell that whatever is behind this door is good.

As you reach out to grab the doorknob, you take a nice deep breath in, and as you exhale, you open the door. It is pure darkness. It is the most comforting darkness you've ever experienced. As you step through the doorway, it's as if you are receiving the most loving of hugs! Take a moment to accustom yourself.

With another big breath, you exhale and notice ten steps leading down. As you slowly move towards these steps, you are amazed at how calm and happy you are in this place. You will now take another nice big breath in. As you exhale, you will start to slowly walk down the steps, counting each one as you go and realizing that this leads to a brightly lit hall with yet another door at the end.

Once you have descended the stairs, you make your way to this door. As you open it, a beautiful, beaming white light streams from this now-open doorway. Step into this light and enjoy its warmth and beauty.

Once you are done, walk back through that doorway and back to the stairs. Turn around to give thanks, then make your way back into your home. Enter your kitchen, closing the door behind you. Take a breath and with the next exhale, open your eyes and start your day. If it is at night that you are using this practice, open your eyes, get yourself comfortable, and drift off to a rejuvenating sleep.

Day One

Day Two

Day Three

Day Four

Day Five

Day Six

Day Seven

May your scales begin to balance as you
lose what weighed on them poorly.

Week Two

Acknowledgement, not Judgment

LAST WEEK'S PRACTICE MAY STILL BE A WORK IN PROGRESS FOR many. You may need to stop and refocus multiple times. This is ok and important to understand that we may feel like we need to force ourselves to sit and learn to focus, to silence, and slow our minds. Still, it's really learning that it's ok not to be constantly consuming, thinking, and processing. As simple as the task may seem, we begin to realize just how scattered our minds can be. Just how judgmental of ourselves we are if we fall off task. How negatively we speak to ourselves about ourselves and our capability to accomplish a task. The most significant factor to consider and remember is that if we tell ourselves we can't, then we can't! If you can catch yourself in this negative self-talk, do your best to acknowledge that you have and are probably setting restrictions within your limitations and abilities. Don't judge yourself but be aware and stay as relaxed as possible.

Ensuring you continue the week one practice alongside future weeks is important, especially during week two. This envisioning of white light will help you filter all that is to come as you continue. It will help you process and accept the self-awareness and acknowledgment that we are working on inviting in. As you sit within this pure and beautiful light, it will not just be helping you with self-awareness; it is also going to be helping you go through and clear yourself of the emotions and hurts that you have stuffed and held within you and ignored. It's like a boost to keep you in it and not get stuck while processing.

Another point that needs to be considered before we continue is what you have been telling yourself so far. If you keep telling yourself that things are a certain way, these tasks are impossible, or that you are just incapable, you won't be able to sit quietly or get yourself to see white. At least not very well. The reason for this is that you've created a belief. This belief will stand strong, and your brain will do whatever sabotage is needed to keep its validity. You will need to recognize these negative beliefs and start getting into the habit of teaching yourself otherwise. You will need to constantly tell yourself that you can and you will. But not just say it, feel it, and believe it.

Don't leave these limiting beliefs unchecked. All they will do is continue with the narrative of "difficult" and "too hard."

This will only stop you from being able to move forward and move on into something happier, brighter, and better. It will keep you low on that emotional scale that was already discussed unless you learn to let go of what does not fill you, of what holds you back. It's important to remind yourself that wherever you are vibrating on that scale, you are inviting all things of that same or similar vibration into your life.

Week two will be filled with acknowledgment of the emotions that potentially have already or will start to surface.

If you haven't already, this is where you may start bringing up old hurts that have yet to be dealt with, or maybe you are just having some realizations or epiphanies about some unhealthy behaviors and habits. In either case, this can cause many emotions and thoughts to swirl in your mind. The focus at this time shouldn't overly be on what actions are coming to the surface but more on what thoughts are going through your mind and how often. Don't get me wrong, these issues will be addressed as we move through these next few weeks together, and working through what's coming to the surface and dissecting it in the most healthy ways is always beneficial. We all know that suppression helps no one, especially in the long run. For severe traumas or issues, seeking professional help is suggested. It can be immensely beneficial when accompanied by a healing practice that fits your needs. If this should be your practice of preference, share this with your specialist, as they can help work through the process and all that will arise.

During this coming week, you must remember to always be easy on yourself. The past can not be changed; the future is always just out of reach, and right now is all we have to work with. If, right now in the present, you can acknowledge moments in the past that maybe weren't the best or played out in a way that would not have been the most optimal for some or all involved and make adjustments for the better of the future without appointing judgment or blame, then you are on a beneficial path for the future.

I want to share my inspiration for week two's task before we get started so that you can hopefully paint a picture of where I want this to take you.

I like to look at the human mind like a filing cabinet, a vast library of filed memories and notes. Some are archived and remembered only by the body; some are placed in a rotation for constant viewing, and so on. The best part of this is that we can replace those files. We can switch them up for our benefit. The first step to ensure the most optimal files are being shown is to acknowledge what's there right now. What is it that you have on replay? What is it that you hold as important or necessary? Are they? Do the opinions, views, and judgments you put so much belief and solidarity in truly benefit you for your highest good? Are they simply a reflection of instilled expectations or fear-based protective shields? A broader and raw deep dive into yourself and what makes you tick is a big step into recognizing what needs to be appreciated for the simple fact of what it is and the expansive learning that came with it and then be replaced with something much more beneficial.

From a young age, we are taught and explained why things are done or not done a particular way, the best way to look, what to eat, how to speak, and so on. All this information is stored in our mental filing cabinets. As we grow, we start to add emotions and traumatic events to these cabinets. Now, this will be different for each, as what one may have taken on as traumatizing doesn't mean it would have been for everyone. It's relative to the person's perspective at the moment it had been experienced. With these impactful moments, we add on self-deprivation and self-blame. The negative expectation of what others would or may say and do if they knew or were to find out. As we look at all of this in a bigger picture, it's essential to start to recognize what was learned, what was expected, and what habits are from others that we picked up along the way. Now ask yourself, was this learned, or was it self-created as experiences occurred and the transmission of information changed? Why did you choose to take on what you did and hold on to it? When things go wrong, or stress starts to mount, what self-sabotaging routine(s) do you fall into? What was your parent's or guardians' "safety net," and how does that affect or alter your decision-making or acceptance today?

Unfortunately for many, it's a negative family pattern they were all sucked into, like a broken wheel that will never correctly turn. The good part is that this is all learned behavior and patterns that can be unlearned and replaced as long as you are willing to look at and answer those tricky questions above and others like: Are these things that our parents said or did? Are these things that you saw? Are these things you experienced? What's going through your mind? How often are you thinking of these things? What's the pattern? If you can link the patterns back to the originating point in time that caused the belief or pattern to be created, they will tell you a great story about yourself.

Now that we have started to think about what makes us tick the way we do, let's go over this week's task.

For this week, you are tasked to be aware of your thoughts each day and do more of a deep dive into their recurrence. Not the thought itself and its deep-rooted meaning, but what do you think about on a weekly, daily, or hourly basis? What is it you are telling yourself as you go about your day? What judgments and opinions are you making/thinking? You need to be aware of all these and how often each one comes up or runs through your mind. What are the most common thoughts and words? Take note of how frequently each occurs. Self-awareness and acknowledgment are crucial to growth. Putting this down on paper so that you can visually see what you have going on and just how often you think of certain things, are making a judgment, whether of yourself or others, or replaying traumatic events can be a big eye opener. The amount of energy you may put towards all of this, is it the best use of your mental capabilities?

You need to see where you are now and have a good and realistic view of that situation to be able to move forward with some healing and understanding. To be able to truly see what it is that you are putting yourself through and how you are restricting and limiting yourself. When you hear people talk about limiting beliefs one has or self-beliefs, these are a set list of created rules and regulations we have placed upon ourselves by the decisions our brain made through the experiences we have had and the information we have absorbed. These rules, regulations, and beliefs can be changed. They can be altered and tweaked so that we can break through the metaphorical barriers built as protection, or so we told ourselves.

Let's break down what is needed to ensure it's fully understood.

If someone walks past you while you are out, and you notice that they are wearing what you believe to be a revealing dress, do you, in that moment, place judgment? Would that judgment, how far it would go, and if it would be vocalized, change depending on where exactly you are and who you are with? And if you think about the thought and/or comment you just had, it truly is a negative one on a matter that doesn't affect you directly. The only reason you have lowered yourself on the emotional scale and, therefore, your energy is that you chose to allow what someone else is wearing to affect you negatively. But why? Did you grow up hearing comments on clothing? Has there been a scolding interaction in the past between your parents or even you and your partner in terms of someone's clothing? Do we feel deep down that we would never be able to wear something like that, and this is potentially the way your envy is escaping? Or maybe it's not about the clothing at all and more about the situation, and the clothing is what you chose to pick on?

The real question in a situation like this has nothing to do with the dress and completely to do with why would what someone else is wearing trigger you into giving the energy away that you did because every judgment placed is just a reflection of your insecurities that are left unchecked. Whether this is a brief thought, an extensive conversation, or somewhere in between, it doesn't matter. The issue is that it was there, and we need to examine why and are these insecurities and fears that we hold knowingly or in our subconscious. When we can catch ourselves in a moment of judgment, whether it be of ourselves or someone else, this is the time to stop and contemplate why? Is this something you are willing to die on the metaphorical hill over, or can you see the thought as something trying to point out a potentially bigger issue within yourself? Even bigger, are you able to look at this inquisitively and not berate yourself for even having had the thought once you start to pick it apart?

Pay attention to how many thoughts like these run through your mind. How much are you triggered or bothered by the views, choices, words, and beliefs of others, and for how long. Recognize when and how often you go over how you disapprove or don't like what others are doing, not doing, or choosing. This is important. Recognize how much you criticize others, judge others, berate others, and, most importantly, yourself! Where's your thought process at? Do you have a traumatic event you're playing on repeat? Is there an event in time you never really got over? Start to pay attention and take notes!

Now, you don't need to physically stop yourself at the moment each time a thought, feeling, or comment occurs but take note for reflection at a more opportune time. Be aware and get it on paper. Look at what you have been focusing on. It's a lot of making sure we are putting the information down on paper so that we can analyze and try to see it from different angles, especially that of the other person or persons. How would you have felt if the tables had been turned? You shouldn't expect or need to see a change in others to feel happy. Do what you need and know what you need for no one else but yourself because those expected changes can be short-lived when requested for all the wrong reasons.

Get those thoughts and words down in your accountability journal for self-reflection (it will also be used at the end of this week). Really become aware of what is going through your mind because, ultimately, we should be able to hold different ideas, beliefs, and opinions from each other. We should be able to hold differing views and opinions from our friends and maintain respect for one another. It's about seeing where you do see agree and showing respect for the rest.

It's one thing to know we are thinking negatively, and it's another to see it all down on paper. To really read it and absorb it in a new way. A second-hand perspective. And if you are finding it too much, you can also make notches for each thought. One header, maybe, and just notches under or beside it for each time it's thought or revisited. This way, we can see, but it doesn't feel as daunting when trying to get it all down before we stop to review it. You could have a column for self-deprecating comments and maybe another for judgment placed on others. This makes it smaller and easier to digest so that overwhelm doesn't take over.

Now if you are completing this with someone, It's not about getting upset when the other tries to point out when they see us in a negative thought. It's not about being able to "one up" each other either by catching the downward spiral. It's about support. Have fun with it. Laugh over it even with each other. Check-in on each other. Be attentive to each other's feelings and notice how you are each affected as you continue. Help point out the shows watched and how they portray how to treat others. Same for music and other absorbable material and information. Pay attention to the people you invite into your world and their effect on you. Learn to not only do better but help each other do better by being supportive accountability partners.

Never stop having more of an overall view and ask where you can better yourself. Where can you go further to do better? Where can you grow? Can you ever feel or have a true sense of accomplishment or happiness if negativity is always running through your mind?

Lastly, as you go through this week, don't forget what's important. Everything happens for a reason. Any time you are placing judgment on anyone or anything, it is a reflection of self. Take note of what thoughts are going through your mind. Don't judge it; just really go through it. How much time are you spending judging and questioning others and yourself? Don't take any of this as a knock on yourself. This can be fun! And think of how much easier this life would be if we were able to not be affected negatively by our surroundings and understand it's a choice. This isn't about ignoring or not having certain feelings or emotions but rather acknowledging them and dealing with them at the moment rather than letting them fester. If we could celebrate even the smallest of victories and accomplishments and learn how to stop that negative voice before it even started to bring us down, our overall mental health would improve. If you feel this might be too much, use the option of daily note-taking. Taking notes for one day and putting those notes away to not be seen again until the end of this week. You could even break it up into morning notes, afternoon notes, and evening notes. The point is to take notes but not focus or pay attention until the week's end. You can do this, and the results will be freeing!

Weekly Tasks

- Imagine white for 10 minutes before going to sleep and before getting out of bed in the morning -Start to be aware of your thoughts and chatter in your mind. What do you tell yourself?

- Take Daily notes on what you think of/play/replay in your mind or tell yourself.
- At the end of the week, before starting week 3, review your past week's notes and take time to review and be aware of the patterns. -Complete the end-of-the-week exercise

Positive Rampage Exercise

You have made it through a week of note-taking on your thoughts and patterns. You will be reviewing and using these notes to reflect on your negative feelings, emotions, and memories to start the process of releasing.

With week two ending, review what you have been focusing on, what has been on replay, what was thought about more than you'd like to see or admit, what self-talk was going on, and what kind of talk or judgment on others was happening. This is all very important in painting a picture of where you are now so that you can know what you are up against and need to work through. Telling yourself that you think you look horrible once a week is easier to process than someone who is telling themselves almost hourly that they are ugly. This constant self-berating creates deep beliefs that will take longer to turn around so that one can truly see the beauty that they possess.

Using your notes from last week, you are now tasked to write down the opposite for each negative thought. An example could be if you call yourself ugly, write down that you are beautiful on a new paper or board, or if you said someone else was annoying for asking questions, try something like others are still learning and questions are good. Think of all the questions you've asked in your life to be where you are or maybe the questions you didn't ask due to insecurities and how this other person must be so brave for being able to speak up and ask. Change these negative judgments, comments, and thoughts into something positive. Create a positive rampage of your own. Make it a list or even a fun pattern. Add color or create organized columns. This will need to be done to suit you specifically so that you want to have it, look at it, and implement it.

Write out this positive rampage in whatever manner makes you happy and will make you want to see it and be able to believe it. Make it concealable if you want so you can bring it with you and use it as a visual reset if you catch yourself in a negative downward fall. It can also be a great visualization of what can be said instead should you be someone that benefits from visual stimuli or coaxing. Start telling yourself these opposites to get away from the negative narrative that you've been working with until now. Say them regularly and often. Say it in your head and out loud.

You could also create a beautiful positive word rampage that consists of all the positives you now have and repeat them to yourself, like your own personal mantra or life statement. This will greatly serve as a support during week 3.

As for your negative notes, make sure you take the time to review them and see just how hard you have been on others and yourself. Take this as an opportunity to see what you have learned up until now and why you want to take on this journey. Take the time to say goodbye to those words, thoughts, and beliefs. Speak to them as if they were a real person right in front of you because, in reality, those words are a part of you. Show empathy and compassion but explain why they need to go and are no longer welcome in your future.

You could safely burn these papers if you would like and visualize this as a release from them. You could rip them up, imagining the breaking of ties with every tear. You can dispose of these in any way you would like and are safely able; however, make sure you acknowledge and separate yourself from them so that you are not bringing them forward.

The subconscious can be difficult to understand, but I assure you that your subconscious takes note when you speak to yourself in the third person with authority on what you want to walk away from and on what no longer serves you. The process is given life, and your will to continue and make lasting changes is boosted. Once this is complete, you are officially ready to start week three!

Positive Rampage Example

I am capable. I am beautiful. I can do this. It may take time, but I will get there. I can find more positive aspects in others. I may have to look harder, but I have decided to take on the challenge with anticipation. I look forward to what road or rabbit hole this may take me down. I'm excited about the doors that have been closed but will start to open as I progress and improve. I know there may be some bumps along the way, and that's ok. Those are going to help me make sure I stay on track. They will come up so I can learn to catch them and be happy for the playful challenge. I will learn to see the brighter side. It may take me some time, and that's ok. I may falter along my path, and that's ok. I will start to learn how to catch myself and stop derailing. I will allow for more play. I will allow for more ease. I will welcome what comes and not assume its direction. I will learn to follow what brings me joy. I will learn to recognize the things that don't more often. I will learn to step away from those things in a healthy way. I can do this. I know I can, and I look forward to congratulating myself when it's done. I look forward to celebrating myself and doing it more often. I look forward to honoring my boundaries. I look forward to putting myself first. I love making sure my cup is always full but not overflowing. I love the contrast of life and the beauty it allows me to see. I love that we can all have differing opinions and still respect one another. I love me. I love everyone else, but I love myself the most.

Day One

Day Two

_____

_____

_____

_____

_____

_____

_____

_____

_____

_____

_____

_____

_____

_____

_____

_____

Day Three

Day Four

_____

_____

_____

_____

_____

_____

_____

_____

_____

_____

_____

_____

_____

_____

_____

Day Five

Day Six

Day Seven

Most live with one eye open, like always
being the passenger in their own car.
The initial double view can be shocking,
but it's worth learning once it's seen.

Week Three

Changing the narrative

Your thoughts and your words bear weight

Now that you have had time to work on and get into a flow of envisioning the white light and having had a chance to focus on what goes through your mind and the thoughts you are thinking, this week will be all about changing that narrative! Catching the negative activity as it's occurring and changing it with no judgment, just acknowledgment and redirection. I hope this past week was a constructive eye-opener on how it doesn't matter what the challenge is; it's about the attitude put forward and how never to berate yourself but simply choose to recognize, learn, and do the best possible. This next week will be on learning to put ourselves to work mentally and not pointing any fingers when we become angry, sad, mad, insulted, etcetera.

Make sure you keep up the white light practice through all of this. The more you maintain a steady practice, the brighter and higher vibrational your life will become.

As for the focus on your thoughts, what conclusions did you come to when reviewing your daily notes? What patterns were you able to see? How judgemental were you of others and their choices? How do you view yourself, and what is it you tell yourself? How often did you say, "I just can't"? How often did you say, "They just can't"? Did you replay that time a parent hurt you? Did you continuously think of that person you fought with and haven't spoken to or seen since? Were you letting small things derail a whole day? More importantly, how judgemental were you of yourself? How much did you hold yourself back because you told yourself you couldn't or didn't have what was needed?

Were you able to see any time when you allowed the actions of others to greatly affect you? Did you have moments where you were thrown into states of anger, frustration, disgust, or other lower vibrational emotions by someone else's views, opinions, or choices? Do you become overwhelmed with the thoughts of what you are telling yourself you need to do or get done? Did your self-expectations cause holdbacks or fallbacks?

If all or any of this sounds all too familiar, it's time to start changing the narrative to create a new perspective.

For this week, the focus will be on paying attention to your thoughts and ensuring we can catch the negative ones before they fully take over and then change them to something more positive. This part starts with the agreement to work on it. To take it on as a challenge or even a game to find the good. This will be about paying attention to the chatter in your head, the gabbing in your mind. It's being able to stop the negative clutter and allow better and more positive focus. You can eliminate that stress and get into an increasingly calm and happy state more and more. It's awareness of negativity, learning about accountability, understanding it, and having it become a focus in your everyday life in replacement of the negative. It's allowing you to catch yourself and question if it's something you need to address now or can put aside till later when you have time to sit with it. Should it be overwhelming or taking over your mind so that you can't continue having a better day, know that the world will continue if you allow yourself moments for focus and reflection.

Now don't think you are expected or should be doing this coming week perfectly. If you can go straight from saying you're ugly too, I'm beautiful and perfect, and truly believe and feel this, then excellent! However, the reality of it is probably that this will take time. It will greatly help that a week has been taken to gather information and patterns in terms of your thoughts and thinking to allow you to get a good picture of where you're starting and where you probably need to be more careful or are ready to change the narrative. Just don't be afraid or worried about starting slow and not running right out of the gate on this coming week's challenge. Remember that pushing yourself for perfection can be negative as well. Perfection can be an unattainable goal as bigger and better continue to creep into view. Set small goals and take a light and playful approach to this coming week. Last week was probably heavy, and some light-hearted game-playing with your thoughts will do you some good.

Let's use the thought of "I'm ugly" as the first example. If you catch the thought of calling yourself ugly in progress, simply stop and change the comment or continue it but positively. You could begin to self-discuss and say, "Yes, that is what I used to call myself, but now I'm working on seeing, finding, and appreciating my beauty." You could also acknowledge the thought and start to call yourself beautiful and feel it and put a smile on your face. Understand that social media has put beauty and "what it is" in a box. Don't stay in the programmed belief that beauty is a certain way. Open your perspective and find beauty in everything around you. I promise it's there and just waiting to be noticed.

Now, if the issue is along the lines of you can't help but say you hate something or someone, try to change it to a positive in any way you can. Hate and the feelings and emotions associated with it are extremely low vibrational. You don't want to attract that to yourself by using or getting lost in it. Not being too drastic with the change could be like, "I might not like that right now, but I'm going to figure out what it is about it that is so triggering for me." This would be important as the judgments we lay out are usually simply a reflection of what's going on internally for ourselves; when you can work on figuring out the why, the irritation of it will start to dissipate. I believe Elon Musk said it best when he stated that freedom of speech was the ability of someone you don't like to be able to say something you don't like, and it is ok. I greatly agree with this, as differing opinions shouldn't be a deal breaker but rather an opportunity for growth.

Let's say the issue is being in a job or place that is negative and causes you anger and frustration, so you've decided to leave. You need to make sure you are settling that negativity so that you aren't bringing it with you to sabotage future opportunities before they even get a chance to materialize or become a reality. In situations like these, sometimes you need to leave quickly. Still, it's always best to change your frame of mind before making the physical change, as the frame of mind you are in is the mindset you carry forward into your next job or place. Try to fix the mindset before the change if you can because if you better yourself first, then better will come. Remember that like attracts like. If you are in a negative mindset, you will attract more negatives. It can be extremely frustrating working with people who express themselves in a way that doesn't truly reflect who they are or if certain levels of integrity, professionalism, or ethics required aren't met. The ultimate understanding is to step away or not give focus to what doesn't bring you joy. If you plan on leaving this employment, use the time left in this place or position to focus on the things you like and enjoy to help bring in a better frame of mind before moving on. If what others are doing is out of your control, The best would be to not give your power away to these annoyances. Your attention is important and shouldn't be given away to any old thought!

Suppose you experienced traumatic events and find yourself replaying them in your mind. You are retraumatizing yourself by mentally placing yourself back in the situation. If you stop and pay attention to how you're feeling in those moments of replaying old negative memories, you will realize, if you haven't already, your emotions are low and negative as you mentally re-experience the event. Changing the narrative or story is a great tool in working through these. You can simply work on changing the outcome. It's not to take away from the event but rather to give your body and mind a break from the hurt and harm you've held onto. The event does not need to reoccur or replay as it had the day it occurred. This time you have the power! It starts with choosing not to retraumatize, anger, belittle, fear-inducing, sadden, stress, hurt, disgust, torment, or torture yourself any longer. Tell yourself that you are taking your power back! Talk to yourself and tell yourself that you are ok, you are safe, you are no longer in danger, you don't need to worry, and you no longer need to self-protect. Know you are no longer the child or person you once were, and confirm to yourself that you are safe as many times as you need. Make sure you know and tell yourself how strong your soul is and how you've already been through it and are now getting past it.

You could also start to change the story as it plays out. Let's use the example of being robbed at gunpoint as the event. If you continue to run the memory or the event through your mind, reliving every detail and how it ended, I bet your physical body is feeling the stress. Maybe not as intensely as the day of the occurrence, but it's there. The next time you catch yourself replaying this memory, change what's happened. If you catch yourself at the part where the robber is running off and about to get away, imagine a police car arriving and catching them. If the next time you catch yourself in this memory, it's at the point of them taking your things; you could imagine that you dropped your possessions and the robber fell over while trying to pick them up and knocked themselves out, giving you a chance to grab your stuff and get to safety. As this continues and you start to catch yourself sooner and sooner within the story, it could turn into seeing the robber walking towards you, but simply asking for the time and continuing. The point is we can't change what has occurred, but we can manage how we will allow it to continue to affect us. Allow yourself to take what positive you can from it. What did you learn? How did it help you grow? How could it enable you to help others? What was once dark can be brought into a beautiful place, and peace can be found. It's a journey that is very much worth the trip.

If the focus is on the people from the past who we feel have wronged us yet we no longer have in our lives, this will be a process of being able to stop the view from pain and hurt and to realign ourselves to see the growth and lessons that relationship had provided. Give thanks for those lessons, and say goodbye to the parts not serving you for your highest good. If we can take ourselves away from moments of pain and look at the situation from a more broad perspective to see the person who had caused the pain, to see why it is that they chose to react the way they did and to try and understand what it is they were feeling themselves at that moment. It may allow us a view of their upbringing, past hurts, and traumas that caused them to be who they were. Maybe they were lost in pain, hurt, and confusion themselves. Now, this isn't excusing the behavior, but to help find understanding in why it occurred, just like documentaries that examine the past and upbringing of someone to give the audience a chance to see that not much else could have been expected from that person. This is meant to allow you to see more to help you move past and not take on other people's choices and actions and carry them like wounds that never heal. It can be a lot, but the more we can sit back and analyze situations to find what helped us, the better off we will be. It's all to learn how to not jump on the emotions that come to the surface immediately. It's ok to get frustrated, but you don't want to be in that emotion for too long. You need to make sure you take moments to breathe and think things over. Especially if it's just too emotionally driven.

A huge "Ah Ha" moment is when we can see situations for more than just the initial thought or perception and recognize the wide variety of angles you could be coming from. Recognize that as you figure out what is right for you, your choice or decision can change as well as that of others, and this is ok. Sometimes we need time to reflect on occurrences or how far is really the healthy length to take something and for how long. Other times you just need to be in it and feel what's coming up, but it can be a fine line between getting through something and getting yourself stuck in it. The best way to avoid this is to detach from expected outcomes and realize that the longer you stay in a negative moment or event or are dragging it out, the longer it will be before something amazing, positive, or great could happen. For this reason, be sure to find a balanced approach and to know when it's time to take a break, when it's time to get it done, and when it's time to get through it so that you can avoid being emotionally derailed or spent.

Remember these important reflections as you complete this coming week's tasks.

It's not about judging or being hard on yourself but simply catching the thoughts and changing them, so recognize that thought and change that narrative. No one can hurt you but you, especially in terms of past events. You don't need to continue traumatizing your body; take your power back. Don't stay in moments and thoughts past their expiration date, and this applies to thought patterns, relationships, jobs, choices, beliefs, and perspectives. Be more curious rather than triggered. Take smaller steps if needed. You don't need to jump right in but don't stay in it or stop moving forward. Showing up can be hard, but it doesn't need to be what we tell ourselves. This comes down to training but more of the mind as the body will follow. It can be hard knowing when to start and stop while in the midst of it, but all that matters is that you do when you can see the opportunity.

Also during this coming week, consider giving yourself some mid-day check-ins for accountability. If you have found yourself falling into old patterns, this will be your chance to get back on track and celebrate even the smallest of your victories. Good luck, and make this week a fun-filled one. It's the beginning of a new mindset that is all about blowing up into positive surprises.

Weekly Tasks

- Imagine white for 10 minutes before going to sleep and before getting out of bed in the morning
- Catch negative thoughts and behaviors and work on changing them into a positive
- Use your positive rampage to help keep you motivated
- Complete the end of the week's exercise - Mirror Practice

The Mirror Practice Exercise

Self-degradation and deprivation can be an issue for so many. I highly recommend taking on this additional practice if this issue affects your life. This is a practice that anyone can implement to have a moment of true soul recognition, but it is something I believe to be an important part of finding love and connection with oneself.

This mirror practice is to help you see all that you have lived through and the knowledge and wisdom it has given. It's to help you see the beauty in your own eyes. To help you recognize the pain and hurts that you've carried. It's learning to see and give love where it's needed the most; to yourself.

There have already been many studies on gazing into another's eyes and the benefits that it can yield. The difference between that practice and this one is whose eyes you will be gazing into. It takes it to a whole other level when instead of gazing into another's eyes to connect lovingly, you're looking into your own. The desired outcome is still the same, the obtainment of love, but it also adds to a realization of how hard you are on yourself and how gentler you need to be. It lets you see the pain in your own eyes. It "clicks" something within yourself to help you look at yourself from a perspective different from what you are used to. It starts to make you question a lot when lovingly doing this practice and genuinely recognizing the person in front of you, who is really just you. It's like looking at someone else who has been through your entire life journey with you and by your side, yet you've neglected and treated them as less than. It is needing to see how you wouldn't do or say these things to others that you do to yourself.

Firstly, you will need a quiet place and a mirror. You will also need paper and a pen/pencil. You'll want to start by writing the most positive things about yourself. The most beautiful things about yourself. Your best qualities, anything positive, write it out. This part is not about the quantity written out but the quality. These are true positives you see in yourself.

Once your list is complete, Get yourself into a comfortable position, set a timer for 2 minutes, and begin to simply stare at yourself. Stare into your eyes for those 2 minutes. Allow everything you see and feel to come to the surface, to come up and feel it, but don't break that eye contact.

After those two minutes, take some extra time to recognize your face and its lines. It's intricacies. See the feelings that this person wears and has carried for too long. Start to tell yourself the positive things that come to mind. Tell yourself all the things you need to hear. Encourage and comfort that beautiful soul that's staring back at you. Allow yourself to be taken to a different place.

At this point, you will need to review the list you made. Recognize just how much you didn't see in yourself. Reflect on the list and restart it. Use the list to remind yourself of how amazing you are and continue to re-evaluate it as you change over time. Continue this practice daily for as long as needed and intermittently when feeling low.

Negative to Positive Examples

Things you may take note of saying and a potential alternative to consider for help as you work on being more positive and changing the negative thoughts into something constructive.

- I'm frustrated with almost everything.
  - o I just need to step away or take a breath before tackling something that initially feels frustrating so that I can really see the potential.

- I do not like what I have to do, and I'm resentful.
  - o Right now might be hard, but I will feel proud of getting through it and the accomplishment once I'm done.

- I hate that I don't know how things will turn out.
  - o I may not know what to expect, and that's ok. I'm working on finding focus on what I do know as the rest sorts itself out.

- The future scares me.
  - o I'm going to focus on the right now. I'm going to love what I've got going on for myself and not even worry about what might be. I will focus on the joy I have for what I'm creating and where I'm going.

- I don't like the person that I am.
  - ○ I'm working on myself and who I want to be, and I'm proud of what I've learned to date because it's all helping me to better understand myself.

- I don't like my coworkers.
  - ○ My coworkers may not be my choice, but I can see what they are good at and grateful for that. They do what they can, and I'll focus on doing my best.

- I don't see value in where I am.
  - ○ I may not understand the value at this moment or experience right now, and that's ok. I'm looking forward to being able to look back at this time with gratitude for what it taught me and how it helped me grow.

- I don't see value in any of what I've accomplished.
  - ○ I've done a lot in my life, big and small. It may not seem significant, but it's all part of what makes me who I am, and there's still time to do more and create more. Everyone has to start somewhere!

- I'm the ugliest person I know.
  - ○ Society may have taught me that beauty is superficial and a certain way, but I'm learning that beauty is everywhere, and I'm working on seeing it in myself.

- I'm stupid and always forget things.
  - o I might not remember everything perfectly, and that's ok. Maybe I'll start making notes or even get myself a nice book or notepad to keep track.

- I hate being alone.
  - o Being alone can be hard, but it's time I need to learn more about myself and what I like and need.

- I am terrible at this.
  - o I may not be the best at this right now, but I will keep trying, and I know I'll get it eventually. Everyone learns at different paces.

Day One

Day Two

Day Three

Day Four

_____

_____

_____

_____

_____

_____

_____

_____

_____

_____

_____

_____

_____

_____

_____

Day Five

_____

_____

_____

_____

_____

_____

_____

_____

_____

_____

_____

_____

_____

_____

_____

_____

_____

Day Six

Day Seven

Lessons are truly learned when
the moments can be released.

Week Four

Finding Joy

A FEW WEEKS ARE NOW BEHIND YOU, AND YOU MAY START TO notice that people see you differently. They may even be asking you what's changed or what has been happening. If they aren't aware of the processes you've been going through and the changes you've been making, they will be able to feel the difference in your energy. Everything is energy, and the energy that one exudes will be recognized and reacted to with like energy as appropriately felt by others around them, whether known or subconsciously driven. If others are feeling and seeing these changes, be sure to take that moment to brag to them about what you have accomplished and are proud of. If they are asking, then they are willing to listen. Moments to flourish in the pride you are entitled to feel are very beneficial and important in staying true to this week's task.

As mentioned above, whatever energy you are vibrating at will attract more of that same energy. That means that as you raise your vibration, you will start to notice those who no longer vibrate at the same level as you start to fall away. The coworker who always came down on you or the neighbor who always picked a fight or had something to complain about, or maybe that relationship with your child or family member that always seemed strained when around each other will all seem just to start to flow with ease. It may not make sense or even happen in a way that will be noticed right away, but the universe will deliver to you that in which you resonate. Perhaps that coworker started working from home, received a new position, or perhaps even left the company. Maybe, the neighbor suddenly changed their schedule or decided to move. Your child is no longer feeling all the tension from you or the expectation of "here comes a fight." They have become less reactive around you. This will take time, but with changes like those you have been working on, your life flow will begin to be one with ease and anticipation.

As for those that begin to fall away or that you seem to no longer "vibe" with, this can be hard to see them as leaving or knowing that this is the end of your experience with them. Letting go can be hard and feel heavy. As you go through this process, know that grief is more than a feeling felt when a loved one passes away. Grief can be felt during a big transition like the ones you may have been through or are starting to go through. If friendships or relationships are changing, just know it's ok to feel the feelings. Give yourself time to acknowledge the relationship(s) for what it or they were and the lessons and beautiful moments they provided. Be sure to let go of what doesn't serve you and not to stay in the feeling of loss. Know that it's ok not to connect or be at the same energetic level as another, but make sure that as you move away from or past that which you no longer feel is for you by continuing to be friendly, wishing them well, and not get stuck again in the disappointment and definitely do not think of yourself as above another. That is another slippery slope that's to be avoided. We are all on our path of learning and experiencing that takes twists and turns and time frames. One is never above or below another. We are all the same, just on different paths.

Stepping away from what doesn't serve you to be able to move forward may be tough at the moment, but the benefits are always well worth the journey. You may feel like you are rebuilding from a whole new foundation at times; however, this is your chance to rebuild with care and attention to the details you had ignored before. This is where you get to be a little more playful and attentive to yourself. It is also an opportunity to figure out who you are now, whom you are looking to become, what you want to bring with you, and what you are ok with moving past or learning what you need to let go of. The universe, during this time, may also give you some extra nudges or experiences to help remind you why you took this journey and to make sure you really are ready to let go of old habits. Perhaps even have something occur to bring attention to what you need to sit with and maybe work on releasing a bit more. Be sure to ask yourself during these testing moments, "Do I really want to keep going with this?" or "Do I really want to keep putting up with this?". You'll also want to stop and pay attention to how those moments make you feel. Again, acknowledge the feelings and know that it's ok to have these feelings and emotions but not to stay in them so that you can continue to expand yourself.

Remember to consider reconnecting to self as you did with the mirror practice and the new level it allowed you to view yourself. Know that when you are feeling stuck or having a hard time letting go, you can always stop and bring yourself back to the mirror. Take the time to stare at yourself in the mirror in these moments to help yourself recognize and console yourself in the way you need. Allow yourself to release and feel safe to do so. If you need, just sit with yourself and cry, laugh, smile, scream, or reflect. Give yourself the time to experience and release all that is needed and be ok with it. This allows you to grow and expand in beautiful ways and become more familiar and accepting of your emotions, and lets them flow. Learn to give your emotions the time they need, but always find your way back to happiness, love, and joy. Send these now-expressed emotions away with appreciation and thanks for what it has sparked within you.

Now it's time to get into a fun frame of mind and even allow ourselves to move towards joy blindly! Submerge yourself into this week's task and the confirmation of what's genuinely sparking joy within you. This means you will have to evaluate and acknowledge what does not bring you joy and what really isn't serving you anymore or in the way you thought it was or how it used to. You are going to have to decide what really makes you happy! It may seem easy, but it can bring up some realizations of past traumas or hurts you never saw coming.

This means you will have to recognize if it's just the joy of others you've taken on. How are you allowing others to treat you, and are you doing things to bring them a joy to maintain the peace or their presence in your life? This means you are merely filling the expectations of others and keeping them happy. You think this is your joy, but it is really the feeling of relief when you are able to keep others happy and at bay.

The expectations of society and your surroundings that you think are your joy may actually be a feeling of being part of something or feeling included by completing what they say or tell you brings joy. This can leave you depleted. Creating boundaries in these situations is essential.

People may be put off at first by this new self-respect and self-consideration, and the universe may even send you a few tests or situations to make sure you are really ready to stick with your new choices and decisions but don't forget how important self-respect is. The beautiful release of these non-serving things from your life and letting them all go allows you to make room for the things that genuinely deserve that space. The recognition of what doesn't fill you up or bring joy and the potential shock that will come with it for you and those around you as you start to say "No" may be unsettling at first, but it will get easier and maybe even start to spark a little light in you as your soul fills with joy from you learning to stay true to yourself. Your ability to walk away from what doesn't or no longer feels right or good to you will indeed feed your soul and bring you joy.

You just need to learn to decipher from what you think you have to do or what should be bringing you joy from what truly sparks something in you. It's the needing to learn how to entirely toss yourself into the choices that bring you joy. Locating these things will require you to get out of your comfort zone and try new places or things. This doesn't need to cost money and can be something free or of minimal cost. Some people find the most joy in being in a forest or down a trail, by being around trees, paying attention to all the details and noises, and speaking to nature. Giving thanks for the beauty and feeling of peace it brings. Some will say hello once they arrive, touch as many trees as possible, and say goodbye before leaving. One could even make it a game to find the most beautiful tree, shrub, or animal along their journey. This not only brings joy by being somewhere you love but adds a playful aspect to the experience. The point is to know "That's my joy!" and to understand that it can be many things, but to have a good grasp on the real joy in your life that is really for you and no one else but you and you alone. It's in a moment of joy, just allowing it to be and immersing yourself in it. It's about not being stuck in survival mode or needing acceptance, or feeling like you belong and missing what truly matters.

You are now tasked to make a list of all the things you feel genuinely bring you joy. This week is all about recognizing true joy versus false perceptions of joy. It would be best if you started by writing out the definition of the word joy at the top of your page. Once you have them all written out, pick them apart! Dissect each one. Why does it bring you joy? Break down if it truly brings joy to your soul or is it because it brings joy to others and makes them happy? It's very important to be kind and help others find joy but also to understand the difference and recognize how much is done for what reason. Was a level of recognition required, or was it simply done for the joy it brought in that moment? These are clues in knowing if something is done merely for the joy it brings or the recognition it gives. Re-evaluate and put consideration of you as you start to review your list. Is it all for you?

If you are simply looking for a self-serving ego boost, you must ask yourself why you need this to feel worthy. There is nothing wrong with self-serving. However, we must ask ourselves if it's to fill our cup or our ego. For this reason, I believe self-serving activities have gotten a bad rap. It's become ok for others to say, "I can't believe how selfish you are." The issue is if it's an activity to fill your soul and take care of you, without recognizing it, they are saying in a way, "How dare you put yourself before me, but don't you dare put this same expectation on me." With some exceptions, the need to feel or be served is unhealthy. We need to ask more questions, such as why it has become socially acceptable to call people selfish for taking something for themselves. Yet, the expectation of having their time and energy put toward others is ok. There is a need to have balance, and this expectation or pointing of fingers is the greatest example of selfishness in itself, as no one should be thinking ill towards another for putting themselves first. In any relationship, mutual respect is essential, but the expectation to carry the weight of another or hold the responsibility for their happiness is unrealistic. This will only create issues as you need to make sure you know what makes you happy for you and brings you joy so that you can enjoy relationships for what they are and as they are and not what one believes they should be getting from it or out of it.

As you continue to create and go through your list, ask yourself if you can acknowledge what makes you happy and brings joy. Are you concerned about what the outside world might think or say? Are you worried about others' opinions or perceptions? Are you putting the weight of shame on yourself from your own beliefs and fears? Are you stopping yourself from fully being able to enjoy yourself out of fear of being belittled or criticized? As you evaluate, remember that authenticity and being true to yourself are a massive part of being able to experience joy to its fullest. The worries you may be taking on can create boundaries and walls between you and your joy.

Once your list is made and evaluated, you will be required to do at least one thing each day this week that brings you joy. This task is essential in understand yourself better and recognize that if you don't take care of yourself, you can't keep giving to those you love and genuinely presenting the best part of yourself. You need to fill your own cup; otherwise, you will simply become depleted and present sides of yourself that no one likes, especially you.

No matter how busy things get or how overwhelmed you may feel on any given day, be sure to find joy in every moment possible. Remind yourself that moments of joy don't need to be anything big or extravagant. The simplest of things can bring you joy. You simply need to learn and acknowledge what you love and make room for it.

You've worked on yourself these past few weeks. You've worked on your mental status. You've worked on your thoughts. You've worked on your self-acknowledgment. You've worked on changing the narrative. You've worked on the inside parts of yourself. Now you will work on ensuring the outside reflects this true "soul medicine" you have implemented.

Here are some healthy reflections for you as you go through this week with joy in your sights. Are you doing things out of true joy, or is it simply expectations from others and society? Are your current joy-filled moments truly bringing you joy or merely filling the cups of others? Always give and show love to others; however, make sure the most is being offered and directed to yourself by yourself. It's no one's job to make you happy but you, so keep raising yourself and be sure to find the beauty and joy in yourself and also just by being with yourself.

Evaluate what you do, why, and whom it's truly bringing joy to. Make sure you are moving away from what you think you have to do, and also ask yourself why you felt that way in the first place. People who are around simply to receive and leave when you start to choose you were most likely around for the wrong reasons in the first place.

The energy that you are putting out is the same that you are attracting. What do you want to put your energy towards?

Nature is amazing and healing. It can really help with healing your body and soul. Are you afraid of something new? Are you afraid of something different? Are you afraid of growth? Are you making excuses to avoid the real problem? It's all choices. Find what it is that's holding you back from jumping in.

Weekly Tasks

- Imagine white for 10 minutes before going to sleep and before getting out of bed in the morning
- Create and evaluate a list of what brings you joy
- Do at least one thing each day that brings you joy
- Complete the additional exercise that follows should you need the release

The Energy Release Exercise

When a situation or traumatic event sticks with you no matter what avenues you tried, and it just doesn't go away, we are fully aware that this is no longer beneficially serving us. It's important to recognize that this is a mourning of sorts. It's a loss. Whether from the loss of someone in your life or the mourning of an event that has stuck with you to the present, there is good and growth that comes from all. When stuck in negative emotions, the problem is how difficult it can become to see or truly embrace them and their benefits.

This lack of ability to fully release can create a held and stagnant energy within you. This stagnant energy can significantly affect your body in many ways. When we are finally able to reach the point of release of these held emotions, we are, at times, also able to experience a change for the better in our physical body. For this reason, it is very important to become familiar with your emotions, the differences between joys and sadnesses, and needs and wants. When we can better recognize and acknowledge our feelings and desires for what they are and simply allow them to be, we are then, in turn, able to release what doesn't serve us better as we encounter it. We are learning to embrace emotions, and sometimes it can take a bit of an extra push to get us past them.

For this practice, You will need to write a letter to yourself. Your pain and your feeling of lack. The lack of emotions. The lack of attention. The lack of love. The lack of desire. The lack in all senses and paths as they were felt. While writing this, you also find yourself tapping into the gained aspects through all that was experienced. Start to write out what you all gained. The learning and the strength. The better, kinder, and loving person it's made you now and for your future. Be sure to be raw and honest. Also, be sure to end this letter by telling "past you" just how amazing and strong you are now. How proud "past you" would be to witness who you are and whom you will become. Give thanks for all that you were and where it's brought you. End this letter with gratitude and optimism for where you are going.

You will need to write a letter like this to any situation and/or persons you can't seem to detach yourself from. Allow yourself to tap into the relationship with that person or moment in time. Allow yourself to really express the ups and downs of the entire experience. Let yourself see where this has allowed you to grow and what benefits it's providing your soul in terms of learning. Give thanks and acknowledgment for the time it has had with you, but it's time to part ways. Allow yourself the time to write out your goodbyes. You could even take moments to see yourself in traumatic moments/scenes that you have held on to. Close your eyes and mentally see yourself in these moments in time. Walk over to yourself and comfort yourself, confirming that this is all over and making sure you let yourself know it and also that you are safe. Hug yourself and show compassion for the strength it had taken to get through these moments.

Before starting this practice, Make sure you have set yourself up comfortably and with support should you need it. Be sure to share with someone trusted that you will be completing a practice of release. This not only allows support for you as you go through this process but also sets the intention of the release taking place and working for your highest benefit. Your vocalization of this process and your ability to embrace it ultimately gives it power. This vocalization will allow the mental process of preparing to let go start before you even get to the physical process. This could be precisely the preparation needed.

Once set up comfortably, write out your letter or letters. Do as many as required. You may also break up this practice into multiple sessions depending on the number of moments you have held onto or the level of impact that had been felt. I also suggest that a letter to self is where you start and finish. Start with the acknowledgment of self, and once you have gone through the release of all that you are finally ready to say goodbye to and move on from, do another letter to check in with yourself and confirm all that you have just completed and how strong you are and where this will take you in the future.

Read these letters out loud. As each one is completed, take the time to read it out loud to give it a voice and confirmation of its completion. As you would read a eulogy at a funeral, read your letter aloud and allow it to be a moment where you are saying goodbye to what's no longer serving you so that you can welcome a more fulfilling and joyful life-filled. Let this be the moment when you finally bring an end to pains you no longer need to carry. Once the letter has been read, rip it up. As you complete this part, be sure you have a smile on your face and are thinking of all that you are grateful for, as well as the release from all that you just expressed. Feel what it's like to finally let go and how much less weight this is on your soul.

Once you have completed this practice, your brain may try to toss in thoughts and memories that bring up these old pain points. What it's doing is not just keeping with the pattern of familiarity but also making sure that you are truly ready to say no more and move forward. As each thought creeps in, be sure to catch it, stop it, and send it off, reminding it that you are no longer giving energy to that which no longer serves you. Your brain will catch up to your newfound joy, and these thoughts will stop. The even better outcome is when you reach a point of not being controlled or tossed into fear and other negative emotions from these thoughts but actually, feel joy in the potential of revisiting them. That you are actually able to see only the good that it provided and completely separate yourself from the parts you felt were negative. This can definitely take time, but it is the ultimate positive outcome.

This practice can be repeated as needed and is suggested as a yearly opportunity to acknowledge what you have completed and what you are looking forward to in the coming year. This is a healthy moment for you to give thanks to yourself for all that you have done and pushed through and speak to the excitement of your future. Understand that everything is for the greater learning and creation of expansion and to allow you to be and to expand beautifully in the life you are in.

Day One

Day Two

Day Three

_____

_____

_____

_____

_____

_____

_____

_____

_____

_____

_____

_____

_____

_____

_____

_____

Day Four

_____

_____

_____

_____

_____

_____

_____

_____

_____

_____

_____

_____

_____

_____

_____

_____

Day Five

Day Six

Day Seven

_____

_____

_____

_____

_____

_____

_____

_____

_____

_____

_____

_____

_____

_____

_____

If you can live like a dog with its head out of the car window, It'll be the most freeing you've ever felt.

Week Five

Evaluating the *"things"*

WHAT I WOULD LIKE FOR YOU TO DO NOW IS REVIEW EVERYTHING you've completed up to this point.

The evaluating of what you've been told and have learned. The evaluation of all the experiences you've had and their effects on your life. The evaluating of your thoughts and where they lead you. Evaluating judgments and views and what serves you and what doesn't. You worked on your energy and seeing where you were versus where you wanted to be. You broke things down. You reinvented yourself as you looked around your internal workings to really understand what truly brings you joy versus what the world around you was saying should be bringing you joy. You evaluated the expectations that were laid on you by those around you. You looked at the things you had to let go of and understood that it's still going to be ok. You learned that it's not a negative thing to be selfish at times and that it is a beautiful thing to enjoy your own company. You learned just how important it is to bring joyful events into your daily life. Most importantly, you finally found your beauty. You learned to love whom you see in the mirror and support that person through this journey.

You will now need to look outside of yourself. You will be looking at your home. The home that you created for yourself to be that safe place and lay your head at the end of the day. I want you to look at what you have created for yourself. I want you to look at all the things that surround you. Look at each item as a representative of an energy of some type that you have welcomed into your home. You intentionally allowed these things to stay and take up space. As you look at each item, whether it meant something to you at some point, holds meaning, was the fulfillment of a desire, was something that was supposed to be of use, something you thought you needed to have per societal expectation, or if it was a gift from someone else, it doesn't matter. What matters is that you have allowed it to stay and be part of your external energy.

It is, without a doubt, a necessity for anyone looking to better themselves and their life to understand that their home is a direct reflection of the state of their mind. For you to continue this journey and maintain it in the most positive and self-supportive way possible, you will now need to look at your surroundings and ask yourself if it reflects the person you want to be or if it is a reflection of pain, sorrow, fear, judgment, expectation, and other emotions we were not able to express or that we instilled on to inanimate objects. Does your home contain things that don't serve you positively, and if they don't, why do you still have them?

You will need to take time to go over all the things you have accumulated. I suggest starting with clearing out the items you know you don't need or want. Start with simple choices. Pack them up, and you could either donate, offer these items to others in case it's something they may need, you could sell the items but with a set date of when it needs to be sold so that it's not kept around even longer, or you may need to throw some items out. Unfortunately, it's a reality if it's broken, damaged, or not donatable.

It'll be easier to get yourself into the clearing and cleaning up process for the more challenging items once you've taken the time to get the obvious not needed or wanted choices moved out.

With a potential vision in sight and the drive to create a home that reflects the you that you have been working towards, keep the momentum going by doing things to keep you motivated, like taking pictures of your space before starting. This allows you to have something to look back on and see how far you've come in those moments when you feel like giving up. It also holds as a reminder of where you once were so that you can look around with pride in the space you have now or are working on creating.

You will have to take the time to ask yourself some tough questions about all that remains. You should also consider these questions when looking to bring new items into your home to avoid clutter all over again. And remind yourself that your home is a reflection of your mind, and you are cleaning it up as well to create a more effortless flow of energy overall. You'll also probably start to be able to see correlations between your home and your mind, like having a cluttered mind means your home is perhaps also cluttered or overfilled. Someone always rushing and racing around probably has a messy home or things constantly out of place. If we can manage to get our house in order, it's like giving our mind an extra helping hand in sorting the internals out.

As you look at each item, ask yourself the following:
Am I holding on to this with the intention of handing it down? And will they, or are they even going to want it?
Am I keeping it because someone said they want me to have it? Would they maybe like to have it back?
Am I keeping it because it was a gift? And why do I feel like I have to keep gifts?
Was it passed down to me? Does someone else in the family possibly want the item?
Would this serve its purpose better with someone else? Is it sellable or donatable?
When was the last time I used it?
Does it spark joy or make me smile when I see it, use it, or wear it?
Does it help simplify a process, task, or job? Is it of great importance to someone else?

If you find yourself holding on to something because it's memory-inducing, try to separate the memory from the item and then ask yourself again if it serves a purpose. It's important to understand that if the item is removed, lost, or damaged, the memory doesn't cease to exist as the memory is not the item. If you realize that you would be better off without the thing, try to see if there's a better way to honor it, potentially by giving it away and allowing the item to serve its purpose with someone else. Perhaps it could be made into a blanket or worked into a piece of art.

If you are concerned with getting rid of an item because of how it was received or from whom you received it, you must ask yourself if the intention of that person was for the thing not to be used and collect dust. Would the person who gave it to you feel happy knowing you are holding onto something that you don't need, use, or even like simply because it was from them? This would be your opportunity to offer it back with a kind explanation of how you no longer need it. It's also an excellent opportunity to sit with yourself and acknowledge that it's okay not to hold on to things out of a believed expectation. You must also ask yourself why you feel this way and understand that the only person you are genuinely letting down is yourself by cluttering your space, internal and external.

If you are simply keeping an item because you don't want to create more waste in the landfill, then it needs to be seen as an opportunity to consider your future purchases to avoid this situation. Understand that nothing can be done further for the items gathered until now. It's better off in a landfill than in your home, creating discontent or simply filling space with no positive intention behind it.

It's also important to understand that holding on to these items costs you. This isn't just monetarily, but it's also costing you your time which is the most important thing you have. You can't create more time, and losing it to frivolous stuff with little to no importance is unfortunate. It does end up coming back to the financial cost of keeping it. Keeping this item in your home causes you to lose time on upkeep, cleaning, and caring for it. You're also losing the space it is taking up in your home. That is space that you pay for. Do you really want to keep paying to house these items or have these items in your life? Our homes are full of cluttered closets, basements, attics, shelves, cupboards, and corners that reflect an unkempt corner of our minds. Whether it's well organized or not, stored nicely or in fancy boxes or bins doesn't provide more value to the items.

If there are things that you are not sure about getting rid of, you can try packing these items up and putting them somewhere to mimic being gone so that you can see how it feels not to have the thing and if it even affects you at the end of a week. You could take pictures of things you thought were important and have the photo to hold onto and reminisce about, but free up space by clearing it, giving it away, or donating it.

Another essential factor to consider with offering it to someone else would be to make sure we aren't cluttering their life with an expectation of them keeping it. This also is important to know not just when rehoming items you no longer want but when gifting to others. Are you buying them a gift to make them happy? Is there an initial reaction of gratitude for the gift, but do they need or want the gift? We need to ensure we aren't cluttering other people's homes with expectations of joy and love. It needs to be acknowledged that love is not an item or a thing. Love is not the material showing or giving of things as society has led us to believe through extravagant Christmases and large wrapped presents at birthdays. Someone's love for you isn't measured by the things they give you but by how they treat and respect you. Love isn't an inanimate object.

This is also an excellent time to evaluate what love truly is for you. Do you say you love things and must have them when shopping? Is this item truly worth the value of love in your life? Do you really, truly, honestly feel love for that thing? If the answer is yes, you must understand that you have just placed the importance of an inanimate and replaceable object at the same level as your pets, your children, your siblings, your parents, your cousins, aunts and uncles, your partner, friends and all whom you hold dear in your life. If you can place the importance of these things within a scale, as we did with the emotional scale previously mentioned, you can begin to see where its actual value rests. An object can hold importance and bring someone joy, but the level of love should be reserved for the people in our lives. Once you've placed an item on the scale of importance, you can now ask yourself if it is truly worth keeping.

I see the word love as an expression of complete and utter contentment and joy. It can be felt when certain people are around, during experiences that have us emotionally flying high, or even when thinking back to moments in time that held great importance and helped shape us. I don't believe love is a thing. I don't see it as an item. You can love the ease that something provides or love the assistance it gives or even the experience it's creating, but we must begin to ask ourselves if we genuinely love these things or if we are simply grateful for what they have provided and understand that they are replaceable.

It's like using the word hate. We might say we hate people. I personally disagree with this view. It is possible to dislike what one is doing, has done, is choosing, has chosen, or even to not understand the how or why. The word hate in itself is extremely negative and very low on the scale in terms of vibration. It's an emotion that can send you into a downward spiral fast. If something is causing you to move in this direction, choose to move the other way. Remember that we choose what we involve ourselves in. It's like a fight; it's only a fight if we also choose to react; otherwise, it's simply a person in discord. Things may happen unexpectedly, but there may not be growth if they don't. We may not like or agree with something and don't always need to. Remembering to take what we can and move forward with gratitude is a practice best remembered and implemented once we can gather ourselves from having experienced an intense situation.

This week will be about focusing on your outer surroundings instead of looking inward and asking if this is how you want to be reflected. Do you need more room, or do you simply need less stuff? You need not get caught up in the moments of "Oh, I need it" or "I need this." Before making your next purchase, ask why you want to get this thing. Do you have to have it? Is it something that will bring joy or ease into your life? Are you buying it to make someone else happy or to feel like you fit in?

Maybe before the purchase, you need to give yourself time to think about why you want it or feel you need to have it. Make sure it isn't just the high of the moment. Ultimately, if it's meant to be, it'll still be waiting there if you decide to leave and go back.

As you are working through defining what is essential and to be kept versus what is to be cleared out, try to separate yourself from the thing itself and why you've held onto it for the time you have. Go with the first feeling felt when you pick it up or look at it. Is it making you happy? Do you enjoy it? Is this something you use daily or weekly? Is it serving a purpose? If you think that the item is something you have to have or should have, be sure to break that thought apart and ask yourself why you feel you have to have this thing, especially if it doesn't fill a useful purpose of some sort in your life. Be sure not to keep things through the assumption of needing them. Think about the last time, or if ever, it was used. Delve deep into the things you surround yourself with and be sure it's there for all the right reasons.

Once things have been cleared, be sure to stop and enjoy the space you have created. Appreciate all the work you've done. Also, look at how your home is emotionally making you feel now compared to how it was before, considering the things you held on to. Congratulate yourself for making room for new memories and experiences by decluttering the burdens of things. See how happy you can be now and how much less time and thought goes into the lack of contentment in your space, whether consciously or subconsciously. You will also be able to see a change in spending when you start being more mindful when considering a purchase.

This may even allow for the ability to do activities or outings that will bring you true joy. Remember that closets and shelves don't need to be packed and full of stuff. Another way to view it is if you constantly need to do big clearouts or spring cleaning, then you are always buying things you don't truly need.

Here are a few reminders for this challenging week of physical work. Instead of spring cleaning, it should be intentional buying. Think about if you need it before you buy it. Be aware of need versus want. Re-evaluate.

Putting sentiment to items creates unhealthy attachments. The thing is not the memory. It's not the memory that leaves, just the clutter.

Don't become lost in fear of the what-if situations. Living in the expectation of a crisis is detrimental. It's the expectation of negative occurrences to come. This will only attract more things to fear or be worried about.

If doing this practice with someone else, be gentle when having an expectation for someone to do this with ease or simplicity in knowing what should or shouldn't be kept as you yourself may be second-guessing items and needing time to ask if it's really something that serves you.

Weekly Tasks

- Imagine white for 10 minutes before going to sleep and before getting out of bed in the morning
- Clear out the things in your home you don't want, need, or like
- Be mindful and take your time in evaluating the remainder of the items in your home -Offer items to others but with no expectations, donate where possible, and toss where needed with the reminder of why you won't want to bring other non-needed items into your life

Day One

Day Two

Day Three

Day Four

_____

_____

_____

_____

_____

_____

_____

_____

_____

_____

_____

_____

_____

_____

_____

_____

Day Five

_____

_____

_____

_____

_____

_____

_____

_____

_____

_____

_____

_____

_____

_____

_____

_____

_____

Day Six

Day Seven

Punish yourself like you would a baby; you are still learning after all.

Week Six

Raising yourself up

ACCOUNTABILITY. ITS MEANING IS PROFOUND. IT IS ONE THING to learn the word. To know how to spell it and its definition. It's an entirely different matter to have to understand its meaning in the sense of applying it to your life in its truest form. Learning and applying accountability to every aspect of your life is challenging but rewarding. It takes a lot of work to look at yourself or view situations from a broader perspective. It can significantly assist in having an easier approach to problems as they occur and towards people and understanding that they are growing and learning along their paths of accountability. It may not be what was expected; however, the challenge itself might have been the look into your own life from a new perspective that you needed.

Always remember that the day will go with the tone you set. A burden or expectation for somebody else is simply guidelines that can be chosen or declined. Criticism is constructive; therefore, your ideals don't need to hold weight for another as theirs don't need to for you, but mutual respect can always be found when the ego is understood.

Make sure that you are taking the time and headspace to be mindful of not just you and your thoughts but also of the things you invite into your space and the people in your life, and those you encounter along your journey. Be sure to set yourself up with things outside of your comfort zone and what you are used to so that you have the opportunity to expand on your list of things that bring you joy. Evaluate the pros and cons of these experiences, and even if it's not for you, take the time to acknowledge what good they did bring.

Be sure to see all the work you've completed. Take the time to see the ups and downs of this journey and where it's brought you. Take these practices from the last several weeks and continue them and keep utilizing them in your day-to-day life. They will help you ensure you have the things, the people, and the thoughts present to all be a beneficial part of your life moving forward. Allow these concepts to help get you through challenges as they arise.

Your only additional task at this time will be to learn to elevate yourself within the white light you've been envisioning. You will simply imagine or see yourself moving up in this white light. See it as a never-ending white that is all around you. Either see yourself moving up the white light or see yourself as if you are watching someone else, moving up and through the white light. As you move up, you are assisting in moving yourself up. You are working on raising your vibration. You are working on releasing energies that no longer serve you. You are inviting more of all that is good into your life.

I wish you the absolute best as you continue along your path. May these practices assist you for your highest good. May you maintain them in your waking life, fall back on them when needed, and share them with others. Find joy wherever you go!

Day One

Day Two

_____

_____

_____

_____

_____

_____

_____

_____

_____

_____

_____

_____

_____

_____

_____

Day Three

_____

_____

_____

_____

_____

_____

_____

_____

_____

_____

_____

_____

_____

_____

_____

_____

Day Four

_____

_____

_____

_____

_____

_____

_____

_____

_____

_____

_____

_____

_____

_____

_____

_____

Day Five

_____

_____

_____

_____

_____

_____

_____

_____

_____

_____

_____

_____

_____

_____

_____

_____

Day Six

_____

_____

_____

_____

_____

_____

_____

_____

_____

_____

_____

_____

_____

_____

_____

_____

Day Seven

_____

_____

_____

_____

_____

_____

_____

_____

_____

_____

_____

_____

_____

_____

_____

_____

_____

Walking into your day with
expectations is like jumping
into shark-infested waters.
Not much good will be found.
Leading with beautiful anticipation is
the best path you'll ever take!

Rebuilding from the rubble

A vision into the journey

Since I can remember, there has been a fear embedded deep within me. This fear drove every thought. Every decision. Every movement. Every attempt to reach out and every pullback. Every day it reminded me that I didn't know what was waiting ahead. What was going to jump out, and what was going to tear me apart?

I lived with this inner fear and outer smile. I felt this knowing that sharing the intimate details of who I am and what I feared, thought, and wished for was strictly forbidden. I feared never being understood and berated further by those I so deeply wanted to fall into.

I needed tenderness and was faced with hard lessons and even harsher words. Being told, I was broken by those who were supposed to fix me. Being told I was unwanted by those who were supposed to love me. Being told I was worthless by those who were supposed to teach me.

I lived in mental torment, contemplating the purpose of my existence, trying to understand what I did wrong. What was it I needed to do to fix where I went wrong?

My fear became augmented with the desire to please but never truly being able to. As I piled on the responsibility for the things that were truly out of my control, I buckled under its tormenting weight.

I had finally hit my low!

I was faced with a jarring decision. I needed to make a choice. I needed to either continue down this dark path that led only to a dead end or choose to dissect what I thought was a sound structure of beliefs I created. It was either the end of where this road could take me or the beginning of a new one that wouldn't be easy at first but had the potential to lead to a brighter path than I ever could have imagined.

This new road would be filled with cut ties and lost friendships and family. It would hold great seclusion to ensure my walls were entirely crumbled so that they could slowly be rebuilt brick by painful brick. I needed to do the hard labor. I needed to figure out what was important to me. What mattered and what needed to go.

The files of my mind needed to be emptied and reassessed for what was truly important and what needed to be shredded after being acknowledged with thanks for the growth it provided. Needing to send out those mental letters letting everyone know that they had been forgiven, for once I could sit and recognize their path; how could I have expected anything different from them?

I wished them all well and continued to rebuild. As my tower grew in size, so did the understanding that I was the only one who truly needed to love me. Others are simply a beautiful complement to this path, and I may have to keep walking past them as I continue to rebuild the walls of my tower and climb its stairs.

My worth, deemed too low for consideration, was being reassessed and determined by me, and I alone. The thoughts I allowed to fill my mental filing cabinets were carefully selected.

I was re-evaluating the bricks that had crumbled in my hands from the past.

I needed to see that the only true teacher I have is myself.

I needed to understand that I chose whose words to take on and whose guidance to follow.

I was responsible for the old tower of hurt that was now in a mess of broken pieces at my feet.

I needed to find myself! And as I continue to work on recreating my tower, I get to decide where the windows will be and where the solid walls will go.

What views will I see out my windows, and what ones will I graciously acknowledge but build past?

It is always a work in progress, but as my tower grows taller, it also grows stronger than ever.

When I need to reassess a section, I do it with kindness and a gentle approach.

I'm new to this construction. I'm new to this journey. I may fall along the way and miss measure, but I know now that I will always have the best company one would ever need.

I'm finally finding that person who was lost long ago.

I will continue the work and make sure I also take my seat in front of that beautiful view of a path I walked once upon a time.

I will smile, knowing I may have tripped over rocks and roots, but it didn't break me. It allowed me to become this fantastic master builder of my tower with new and even more beautiful moments and people to help me enjoy it.

With each brick and added step, I will learn to love and give love. I will be joyously me!

Last time it was this; now, it is that.
You need to stop giving me this
and that and start coming forward
with something more tangible!

Printed in the United States
by Baker & Taylor Publisher Services